A Gift For:

_____

From:

How to Use Your Interactive Story Buddy™ :

1. Activate your Story Buddy by pressing the "On / Off" button on the ear.
2. Read the story aloud in a quiet place. Speak in a clear voice when you see the highlighted phrases.
3. Listen to your Story Buddy respond with several different phrases throughout the book.

Clarity and speed of reading affect the way Abigail™ responds.
She may not always respond to young children.

Watch for even more interactive Story Buddy characters.
For more information, visit us on the Web at Hallmark.com/StoryBuddy.

Copyright © 2011 Hallmark Licensing, LLC

Published by Hallmark Gift Books,
a division of Hallmark Cards, Inc.,
Kansas City, MO 64141
Visit us on the Web at Hallmark.com.

Editors: Emily Osborn and Megan Langford
Art Director: Kevin Swanson
Designer: Mary Eakin
Production Artist: Dan Horton

ISBN: 978-1-59530-359-2
KOB8024
Printed and bound in China
NOV12

Hallmark's I Reply Technology brings your Story Buddy™ to life! When you read the key phrases out loud, your Story Buddy™ gives a variety of responses, so each time you read feels as magical as the first.

BOOK 3

ABIGAIL
AND
The Lost Purse

Hallmark

By Lisa Riggin

Illustrated by
Lynda Calvert-Weyant

Some little girls can't wait to grow up—and
Abigail was one of them. Once, when Abigail was
really little, she turned the hands of a clock ahead
to see if she could grow up faster!

Even if she couldn't be grown-up right away,
Abigail loved doing grown-up things.

Today Abigail was cleaning her room. She collected all sorts of things she didn't use anymore. She made stacks of books and games and toys to give away.

She found a tutu that was too-too small and added it to a pile of clothes. Looking at everything she'd gathered, she told herself, "Abigail, you're doing a great job!"

Before cleaning out the dresser, Abigail decided to put all of her favorite necklaces into her purse to keep them safe. But her purse wasn't in its usual place on the hook!

Abigail looked in her closet. She checked behind the door. Abigail looked but couldn't find it.

Abigail's mom heard the commotion coming from Abigail's room. When she got there, she could see that Abigail was upset.

"I can't find my purse anywhere," Abigail said as she flung books and scarves behind her, looking for it. "It's a disaster!"

Abigail's mom said they would look for the purse together. "Can you remember the last time you had it?" she asked.

"I was in the living room reading yesterday, and I know I had it then," Abigail said, starting to calm down. Abigail always felt better after talking with her mom.

Abigail and her mom looked behind and under the sofa and cushions, but the purse wasn't there. But they did find a couple of frilly boas Abigail was wearing yesterday.

Abigail wondered if her purse might be in the bookcase.
Abigail looked but couldn't find it.

"Let's keep looking," said Abigail's mom, and the two of them checked the front hall closet. They didn't find the purse there either. But when they saw themselves in the mirror, they decided to put on hats to go with the boas.

Abigail thought they looked terrific!

The next place they looked for the purse was the basement playroom. "It has to be there." Abigail checked the toy chest in the corner. The purse wasn't there. She opened drawers and checked in boxes.

Abigail looked but she couldn't find it.

Abigail's mom didn't find the purse either, but she did find a couple of fancy dresses to go with their hats and boas.

"I think we look wonderful," said Abigail, "and I look so grown-up!" Abigail loved doing grown-up things!

"Now all we need are some high heels to strut our stuff,"
said Abigail's mom.

"I know where we can get those!" Abigail led her mom
upstairs and to her room.

Abigail wiggled under the bed and pulled out the big box of
old clothes stored there. They dug through the box until they found
two pairs of shoes that seemed just right.

"These are perfect!" they both said, trying them on. Posing
in front of Abigail's mirror, they admired the view. Abigail thought
they looked terrific!

"The weather's lovely this time of year, don't you think?" asked Abigail's mom in her very best lady voice.

"Oh, quite," laughed Abigail, trying to sound like the Queen of England.

"You know," said Abigail's mom, "outfits like these should be seen. Let's walk to the ice-cream shop and show them off."

That was all she needed to hear! Abigail was very, very excited.

"I just need to get my necklace," said Abigail. She ran to her room to grab the locket from the dresser. And there was her purse—sticking out of the top drawer!

"Now I'll really look like a lady!" Abigail couldn't help but smile.

On the way to the ice-cream shop, the two very proper
ladies waved at neighbors and wished them a good day
in their very best lady voices.

At every window, they checked their reflection to make
sure their hats were still on straight. Abigail thought they
looked terrific!

"It's fun being a lady with you, Mom," said Abigail. And as she slurped up the ice cream melting on her cone, Abigail beamed with delight!

Did you have fun reading with Abigail™?
We would love to hear from you!

Please send your comments to:
Hallmark Book Feedback
P.O. Box 419034
Mail Drop 215
Kansas City, MO 64141

Or e-mail us at:
booknotes@hallmark.com